Accepting the Disaster

FARRAR STRAUS GIROUX NEW YORK

JOSHUA MEHIGAN

Accepting the Disaster

Joshua Mehigan's first book, *The Optimist*, was a finalist
for the 2005 Los Angeles Times Book Prize in poetry.
His poems have appeared in many periodicals, including
The New Republic, *The New York Times*, *The New Yorker*,
The Paris Review, and *Poetry*, where he has been a
frequent contributor of poems and essays. His writing
has also been featured in *Poetry Daily* and *The Writer's
Almanac*, and in numerous anthologies. He is the
recipient of *Poetry* magazine's 2013 Levinson Prize
and of a fellowship from the National Endowment
for the Arts. Mehigan lives in New York City.

ALSO BY JOSHUA MEHIGAN

The Optimist

Accepting
the
Disaster
Joshua
Mehigan

Farrar, Straus and Giroux
18 West 18th Street, New York 10011

Printed in the United States of America
Published in 2014 by Farrar, Straus and Giroux
First paperback edition, 2015

The Library of Congress has cataloged
the hardcover edition as follows:
Mehigan, Joshua, 1969–
  [Poems. Selections]
  Accepting the Disaster / Joshua Mehigan. — First edition.
    pages cm
  Includes bibliographical references (p.)
  ISBN 978-0-374-10098-8 (hardcover)
  I. Title.

PS3613.E425 A6 2014
811'.6—dc23

                                        2013034991

Paperback ISBN: 978-0-374-53546-9

Designed by Quemadura

www.fsgbooks.com
www.twitter.com/fsgbooks
www.facebook.com/fsgbooks

1 3 5 7 9 10 8 6 4 2

FOR TALIA

Contents

Accepting the Disaster

Here

Nothing has changed. They have a welcome sign,
a hill with cows and a white house on top,
a mall and grocery store where people shop,
a diner where some people go to dine.
It is the same no matter where you go,
and downtown you will find no big surprises.
Each fall the dew point falls until it rises.
White snow, green buds, green lawn, red leaves, white snow.

This is all right. This is their hope. And yet,
though what you see is never what you get,
it does feel somehow changed from what it was.
Is it the people? Houses? Fields? The weather?
Is it the streets? Is it these things together?
Nothing here ever changes, till it does.

The Smokestack

The town had a smokestack.
It had a church spire.
The church was prettier,
but the smokestack was higher.

It was a lone ruined column,
a single snuffed taper,
a field gun fired at heaven,
a tube making vapor.

The smoke thinned the attention.
Its aspect kept transforming.
It could look like a cloud, or like
mosquitoes swarming.

The smokestack's bricks were yellow,
and its mouth twenty feet wide.
Its smoke was usually pale,
but there was a rust color on its side.

The smoke was yellow coral,
a bouquet of yellow roses,
a yellow beard, a yellow eye,
and sometimes runny noses.

Often it looked heavy
like junipers under snow.
At dawn it was limpidly pink
and shaped like an embryo.

It could look like Cuba
as seen from outer space.
It could look like a pedestal stone.
It could look like Jesus' face.

The busy residents
tended to ignore it,
though no one alive remembered
a time before it.

Sometimes it looked like ermine,
sometimes like elderflower.
Sometimes it looked like a Persian cat,
and sometimes like power.

It came before Lincoln Steffens.
It survived Eric Blair.
It was older than stop signs.
It would always be there,

resembling a tuxedo ruffle,
or an elephant head,
or a balled-up blanket
on a hospital bed.

It stopped three times a year,
but only for one day.
Once, in the '30s, it seemed to die.
Many families went away.

But it stayed dead a week,
and when it was resurrected,
the sky turned black, and then white,
as if a new pope were elected.

To labor it looked like a witness,
to management a snitch,
to both victim and perpetrator
it looked like getting rich.

At the Chamber of Commerce,
on a postcard of the square,
you'd find it in the background,
diminutive but there.

On cool summer evenings,
it billowed like azure silk.
On cold winter mornings,
it spread like spilled milk.

Fire Safety

Aluminum tank
indifferent in its place

behind a glass door
in the passageway,

like a tea urn
in a museum case;

screaming-machines
that dumbly spend each day

waiting for gas or smoke
or hands or heat,

positioned like beige land mines
overhead,

sanguine on walls,
or posted on the street

like dwarf grandfather clocks
spray-painted red;

little gray hydrant
in its warlike stance;

old fire escape,
all-weather paint job peeling,

a shelf for mildewed rugs
and yellowing plants;

sprinkler heads,
blooming from the public ceiling;

all sitting
supernaturally still,

waiting for us to cry out.
And we will.

The Sponge

None of us understands our story better
than this nonentity, unconscious slip
of nature, nonetheless our common parent
dilating at the bottom of the sea.

The parent, too, of octopus and pony,
of reefs and villages, once it was strange
simply for being not a rock itself—
not rock, but a blank sleep on a rock shelf.

And, deeply sympathetic to the rock,
to sea and sea dust washing through its skin,
it knows, although it doesn't know it knows,
that minds and their milieux are all one thing.

Some see its way of thinking; most, not yet.
Still, one day, just by living, all will find
reason enough within themselves to think
the single thought forever in its mind.

The Crossroads

This is the place it happened. It was here.
You might not know it was unless you knew.
All day the cars blow past and disappear.
This is the place it happened. It was here.
Look at the sparkling dust, the oily smear.
Look at the highway marker, still askew.
This is the place it happened. It was here.
You might not know it was unless you knew.

The Cement Plant

The cement plant was like a huge still
nailed in gray corrugated panels
and left out forty-five years ago
in the null center of a meadow
to tax itself to remorseless death
near a black stream and briars, where
from the moment it began to breathe
it began falling apart and burning.
But it still went, and the men were paid.

The plant made dust. Impalpably fine,
hung in a tawny alkaline cloud,
swept into drifts against mill-room piers,
frozen by rain on silo ledges,
dust was its first and its final cause.
Pinups were traced on their car windshields.
Dust gave them jobs, and killed some of them.
Late into evening their teeth grated.
Its product was dust, its problem dust.

The thing was blind to all its own ends
but the one. Men's ordinary lives,

measured out on a scale alien
to that on which its life was measured,
were spent in crawling the junk machine,
fitting new gaskets, screws, and bearings,
deceiving it toward the mood required
for it to avail and pay. Somehow
it did. None cheered it. It sustained them.

The Hill

On the crowded hill bordering the mill,
across the shallow stream, nearer than they seem,
they wait and will be waiting.

Rain. The small smilax is the same to the fly
as the big bush of lilacs exploding nearby.
The rain may be abating.

On the quiet hill beside the droning mill,
across the dirty stream, nearer than they seem,
they wait and will be waiting.

The glass-eyed cicada drones in the linden draped like a tent
above three polished stones. Aphids swarm at the scent
of the yellow petals.

A bird comes to prod a clump of wet fur.
The ferns idiotically nod when she takes it away with her.
Something somewhere settles.

On the crowded hill bordering the mill
is our best cemetery, pretty, but not very.
All are welcome here.

Sun finds a bare teak box on the tidy green plot.
It finds lichen-crusted blocks fringed with forget-me-not.
Angels preen everywhere.

On the crowded hill bordering the mill
is our best cemetery, pretty, but not very.
All are welcome here.

Joe Pipe

The black cowboy hat
with buffalo-nickel trim,
the fine nose and mustache that sat
under the wide brim
like a dopey disguise,
and, out of sight of the sun,
the black button eyes
fixed far ahead of him
in deep thought, or none:

that man was something to see,
one large boot, also black,
up on his delicate knee
as he spread out and settled back
on a park bench or, standing to go,
raised to his ear again
the dumb radio
with the hole at the back
where the batteries should have been;

or at the bowling alley,
in awkward company
of others like him—though really,

hatless and bootless, he
might be their overseer,
sliding to a full stop like
a bright Olympic skier
in a lip-balm ad on TV . . .
and, after, the rumbling, the strike;

then the shoe desk, and one beside him
to help with left and right;
and outside, from his vest, the star item,
brought matter-of-factly to light:
the pipe, trick answer to
the question of his face,
hung like the tail of a Q
from his solemn overbite
as though books and a fireplace

awaited somewhere, though
his pipe was less plausible than
even the radio,
being plastic. Good if that man,
who would have no spouse or car,
could feel that a toy, along
with the clothes and the boots that he wore,
made him like other men.
Also, he was not wrong.

The Forecast

Here nothing moves across the even sky,
and nothing moves the mile of dusty corn.
Nearby, the red house sleeps beneath a tree,
the house he put there, near the pine he planted
some past September, waiting for the weather
and corn to work out all the final details.

March lion.
March lamb.
April showers.
May flowers.
Soon June's
soft scion.
Then August's
battering ram.
October sours
May bowers.

Down in the Valley

It was her first time coming home from college.
She headed downtown for a drink or two.
Her girlfriend went home early. That was Christmas.
Now, under sapling pine trees in the clearing,
snowdrops are coming back to their old places.
They had been gone a lifetime. Now they stand,
poised like a choir on the verge of singing:
Nature is just. There's nothing left to fear.
The worst thing that can happen happened here.

The Fair

The fair rolled into town surprisingly
intact, like a plate unbreakable because
it has been dropped and glued so many times
that it is all glue and no plate. The fair
was no fair. But, oh, it was a thrill!

The fair slid into town just as a clown
slides into pants. The fit was loose but right.
The sheriff had a job directing traffic.
The barber was the sheriff for a night,
and people paid to see a human ape.
They frowned to find her happy and alive.

The fair spilled into town like a box of tacks.
Later that month, in with the rest at church,
were people no one knew,
though none could tell exactly who was who.

Work Song

This fastening, unfastening, and heaving—
this is our life. Whose life is it improving?
It topples some. Some others it will toughen.
Work is the safest way to fail, and often
the simplest way to love a son or daughter.
We come. We carp. We're fired. We worry later.

That man is strange. His calipers are shiny.
His hands are black. For lunch he brings baloney,
and, offered coffee, answers, "Thank you, no."
That man, with nothing evil left to do
and two small skills to stir some interest up,
fits in his curtained corner of the shop.

The best part of our life is disappearing
into the john to sneak a smoke, or staring
at screaming nonstop mills, our eyes unfocused,
or standing judging whose sick joke is sickest.
Yet nothing you could do could break our silence.
We are a check. Do not expect a balance.

That is a wrathful man becoming older,
a nobody like us, turned mortgage holder.
We stay until the bell. That man will stay
ten minutes more, so no one can complain.
Each day, by then, he's done exactly ten.
Ten what, exactly, no one here can say.

Elegy

Yes, we were kind, and brave, and honest once.
Beige foyer to tan restroom to beige chapel,
the fifty folding chairs, the eighteen people,
and, somewhere, him. My suit coat pulls my shoulders.
Monica, Bob, Amanda, Mike, and Pam,
how terrible to see you all again.
The reverend, too: an incorrect assumption.

And, laid apart beneath the track lights, what?
Collarless white tuxedo shirt. A mullet.
The unimaginably bad foundation.
Comic books, slipped in by his long-lost father,
whom someone told his son liked comic books.
A small laugh, burning nose, and in my eyes
a little water. Home. Feet somewhat sore.

Later tonight, the full cost being paid,
we gather in a dark place outside town
and, in accordance with his simple will,
Monica, Pam, Amanda, Mike, and Bob,
Pistol and Doll, Shadow and Rumour, and I
drink up what little money he had saved.
And now we're mean. We're terrified. We lie.

On the Way to Church School

The girls and boys
that stammer by
at one o'clock
stretch half a block.
Clouds follow them;
also, the steeple.

The tallest and others
waiting to see
what the tallest will do
tie parkas of blue,
yellow, or red
around their waists.

Already lost,
one boy had tied
a parka of red
around his head.
That boy now lies
shoved on the grass.

Ms. Bell, who ably
shepherds them,
and Mrs. Stack,
in the way-back,
coolly chide
but do not holler.

The smallest pause
with giant eyes.
The sidewalk glints
at the innocents
so like people
only smaller.

Sad Stories

Don't stop 'til you get enough. MICHAEL JACKSON

No one is special. We grow old. We die.
In silk pajamas, in a pretty morning
glimpsed through Venetian blinds, joy even now
might sometimes visit as it used to. Bright
hillsides of early June, mockingbird song,
the highest button of your shirt undone;
a road along a beryl stream, both glinting,
the road already warm, the stream still cool—

I met a barmaid once whose fingernails
were very long and varnished white. Years later,
I saw her at a restaurant. She'd gained weight.
Gathered around her eyes was disappointment.
From almost every fingertip, as long
as if she'd nurtured them that whole time, grew
a varnished claw, curved inward, like a sloth's.
Couldn't she see how those betrayed her most?

Somewhere your true love walks ahead of you.
And, every day, your injured scarecrow's face,

threadbare disguise, recedes. The surgeon says,
"Sometimes the enemy of good is better."
Who hasn't seen your eyebrows answering always,
"We are amazed"? Your widening sanguine eyes
or noble jaw, past pride and compromise?
Botulin, hydroquinone, alkalis—

I knew a man, once, in his early eighties
who in his teens had danced for Balanchine.
He was a brilliant raconteur and gossip,
and we tried not to stare at the toupee
laid on his head like rusty steel wool.
Which of us could have told him? Then, one night,
we saw a picture from a newspaper,
Paris, June '39, himself onstage,
beautiful, in a tour jeté.

                    Outside,
a zodiac of poison eyes is rising.
The mobs that cheer beneath your balcony
are dying to be you; you're dying not to.
Bright children wonder what it's like to be
the child of a macabre emergency
locked in a lavish room above the city—
paradox and cliché of royalty.

I saw a movie once about a prince,
extravagant like you, like you eccentric.
But he became a savage autocrat,
ordered the sun to rise, and raped his sisters.
One bust portrays him in his musculata,
with empty eyes, but also with the injured,
sensuous lips and forehead of a boy.
"Remember only what you leave behind,"
the young prince might have counseled you. "And when

our life, this passing unendurable fever,
a world of pain, a glint of joy, is done,
bejeweled, in fine silk, you will emerge a god."
He dreamt, one January, that he stood
in heaven by the throne of Jupiter.
Then, suddenly, he felt the god's right boot,
then felt the earth against his cheek, then woke.
The following day, his own guard murdered him.

Father Birmingham

Do you remember Father Birmingham
telling about the Sacrificial Lamb,
his little voice gigantic in the nave?
His septum looked like skin inside a pepper.
He loved the tale of Damien the Leper.
He stressed good works and giving, and we gave.

Bottomless glasses that, removed, laid bare
a foggy, oddly vulnerable stare,
his red, lined neck that smelled of aftershave—
sure, I remember Father Birmingham.
He's an important part of who I am.
He taught me not to be but to behave.

The Bowl

For weeks, the heavy white ceramic bowl
he left out back lay tilted to one side.
But then one morning it had been put right.
Was it the possum, called down late at night
by hunger from some bony treetop? No.
The possum only ever tipped it over.
But when a small bird perched to drink from it,
he laughed, remembering all night long the rain
dashing across the gutters and the roof.
The bowl was full. The rain had righted it.

At Home

. . . very few are able to tell exactly what their houses cost . . . THOREAU

This is my lawn. I planted it, I grew it,
and I work hard ensuring it's attractive.
I keep it clear of every type of pest.
I rake it and I mow it. I see to it
that no stray dogs stray here. It keeps me active.
God sends the sunshine, and I do the rest.

That is my fence, where I go lean to eavesdrop.
Outside of my own thoughts, I hear the quiet
of many smaller creatures barely moving.
In the fall, sometimes I can hear the leaves drop.
My land is mine. I have worked hard to buy it.
It's one thing I can always be improving.

In it, I find it's easier to find
the natural boundary of my heart and mind.

Citation

Their ruler is elected state by state,
and no one cuts his heart out as he drowses.
Their senior citizens still copulate.
Their convicts are allowed to change their blouses.

In this back yard there hangs a gutted deer,
and in that driver's seat there sits a wife.
They have their MMR and Retrovir.
They have their quarter-century more life.

Each commoner receives a welcome mat.
The maids have maids, and plumbers go to Paris.
They call their waiters "sir." The poor are fat.
They eat. They do not easily embarrass.

Epitaph Carved on a Shinbone

This man was not like others. Others work,
others have plans. Nobody knew his plans.
We watched him at the market or the park,
making his way without us, without friends.
That night, his sheepdog didn't growl or bark.
The door was open. He didn't raise his hands.
This man was proud, and different, and withdrawn,
too quietly, in his own way, outside town.

Cold Turkey

They're over now forever, the long dances.
Our woods are quiet. The god is gone tonight.
Our girls, good girls, have shaken off their trances.
They're over now forever, the long dances.
Only the moonlight, sober and real, advances
over our hills to touch my head with white.
They're over now forever, the long dances.
Our woods are quiet. The god is gone tonight.

The Dream Job

He slid the new flights on and lined them up
and tacked them on and started welding them.
He went to take a leak and came right back
and then he slid the collar on the barrel
and set the indicator on the collar.
He rolled the barrel twice and got the reading,
six thousandths out, then marked it with the soapstone.
He stuck the ram in underneath and pumped,
then let it sit, then turned the knob. It settled.
He clocked out, showered, and drove the hour back home,
then kissed his son, then kissed his wife, then sat.
He ate his cube steak and he drank his milk.
He watched the news and then whatever followed.
Then it was bed. He lay there in the dark
and smoked a cigarette. He kissed his wife
and closed his eyes and sank and got the reading,
three thousandths out. He pumped it up again,
a thousandth over, then backed off the knob.
It settled. That was done. He got the torch
and cut the flights, and got the hardface out,
hardfaced it, checked it over for low spots,
then, finally, sent it up to Harold. Then
they brought another. Then he woke for work.

Psalm

Grant me, Lord, the wretchedness
to attribute each success
wrung from air with strength and skill
to your paranormal will

and to credit grief, disease,
poverty, catastrophes,
shortfall, pain, and death alone
to some failing of my own.

How Strange, How Sweet

This was a butcher. This, a Chinese laundry.
This was a Schrafft's with 10-cent custard ice creams.
Off toward the park, that was the new St. Saviour.
Then, for five blocks, not much but chain-link fences.
These foolish things, here today, gone today,
yesterday, forty years ago, tomorrow.
Doloreses and Normas not quite gone,
with slippers on, and heads like white carnations,
little, and brittle, and mum, why did the fine
September weather call you out today?
To dangerously bend and touch a cat.
To lean beside your final door and smile.
To go a block and get a thing you need.
What are you hiding, ladies? What do you know?

Micks were from here to there. Down there, the Mob.
And, way down there, the mob the bill let in.
Far west were Puerto Ricans. Farther west,
in Newark, Maplewood, or Pennsylvania,
one canceled choice away, why, there's nostalgia,
lipstick, and curls, and gum, and pearls on Sunday.
So here's a platinum arc from someone's neck chain,

bass through a tinted window, loudest laughter,
the colored fellow with the amber eyes
who doesn't need to stand just where he is.
Here sits the son of 1941,
a pendulous pink arm across a chair back;
his sister, she of 1943,
her hair the shade of an orangutan.
Food stamps and welfare, Medicaid and Medicare.
Kilroy was here. Here was where to get out of.

Last come the new inevitable whites.
See how the gracious evening sunshine lights
their balconied high-rise's apricot
contemporary stucco-style finish.
Smell the pink-orange powder as some punk
sandblasts Uneeda Biscuit off the wall.
Flinch at the miter saw and nail gun,
at three-inch nails that yelp as men dismantle
a rooftop pigeon loft. Those special birds
will not fly home to the implicit neighbor,
or fall like tiny Esther Williamses
in glad succession from a wire, to climb
and circle in the white December sky.
Far up, from blocks away, the pale birds seemed,
when they all turned at once, to disappear.
Across the street, the normal pigeons eat.

Heard at the Men's Mission

How many sons-of-bitches no one loves,
with long coats on in June and beards like nests—
guys no one touches without latex gloves,
squirming with lice, themselves a bunch of pests,
their cheeks and noses pocked like grapefruit rind—
fellas with permanent shits and yellowish eyes
who, if they came to in the flowers to find
Raphael there, could not be otherwise—

have had to sit there listening to some twat
behind a plywood podium in the chapel
in a loose doorman suit the color of snot,
stock-still except his lips and Adam's apple,
telling them how much Jesus loves the poor
before they got their bread and piece of floor?

Try

Her unconcern with everything including the complicated smile
    and dropping jaw of Mama Cass up front at Monterey.

Her violently pumping on the balls of her forgotten feet, and
    under them the kitten heels unmoving on the stage.

Her, before Gloria Swanson, on Dick Cavett.

Her psychedelic Porsche, someday the Whitney's, still in the
    motel parking lot at one.

The Polling Place

Same place as four years ago. The people arrive
tired by daytime. Nighttime is ten after five.

The flag is lit, and the sculpture of who knows who.
Here's the fire door, wedged open with *Voting and You*.

From inside, a floor-wax smell. Shy people come after.
I walk past them into bright light and social laughter.

This could be Bingo. It could be a 12-step meeting.
It could be a bake sale. I could be home eating.

The bathroom is closed to all but volunteers.
Democracy is slow. It can take many years.

Somebody's takeout cancels the floor-wax smell.
I could be eating and doing laundry as well.

Suppose the will of the people was as heavy
as our bag of laundry out in the back of the Chevy.

Measured on that scale the will of the person counts
a fraction of a fraction of an ounce,

and if that's correct my will is not very strong.
Still, if the right one wins I was right all along.

The bathroom is closed to all but volunteers.
Three tons of dirty laundry is made in four years.

Today my will is the weight of a grain of salt.
But then if the wrong one wins it's not my fault.

The Professor

I get there early and I find a chair.
I squeeze my plastic cup of wine. I nod.
I maladroitly eat a pretzel rod
and second an opinion I don't share.
I think: Whatever else I am, I'm there.
Afterwards, I escape across the quad
into fresh air, alone again, thank god.
Nobody cares. They're quite right not to care.

I can't go home. Even my family
is thoroughly contemptuous of me.
I look bad. I'm exactly how I look.
These days I never read, but no one does,
and, anyhow, I proved how smart I was.
Everything I know is from a book.

The Library

We have all been there once. Some, more than that.
They forced us all to visit one September.
But that was such a long, long time ago.
There wasn't anything to marvel at.
The door was heavy. That I still remember.
Inside were many things I'll never know.

The Orange Bottle

The clear orange bottle was empty.
It had been empty a day.
It suddenly seemed so costly
and uncalled-for anyway.

Two years had passed. They had passed
more or less the way years should.
Maybe he'd changed. Or maybe
the doctors had misunderstood.

It was June. The enormous elm tree
was green again, and the scent
of hyacinth reached through the window
and followed wherever he went.

And the sky was the firmament!
His life was never better.
Each small white spotless cloud that passed
was like a long-wished-for letter.

But then he remembered his promise.
It came like a mild cramp,

and it sat there all day in the back of his mind
like a gas bill awaiting a stamp.

He saw three faces that Sunday,
mother, sister, niece,
all with the same kind, brown, scared eyes
that brought him no peace.

The sidewalk sparrows were peeping.
His whole house smelled like a flower.
But he remembered his promise.
The drugstore said one hour.

Back home again, he was tired.
The label said caution, said warning.
He left the clear orange bottle
on the lip of the sink till morning.

The insert said warning, said caution.
The insert said constipation.
It said insomnia, vivid dreams,
and hypersalivation,
    and increased urination,
    and a spinning sensation.

It also said night sweats, and
agranulocytosis,
and strongly suggested a full glass of water
be drunk with all doses.

The insert said all this,
the insert he never read.
But he didn't have to read it
to know what it said.

The bedroom was calm with moonlight
and the breeze through the screen was cooling.
Through the elm leaves the shivery light on the wall
came like quicksilver pooling.

But just before five, something woke him—
a close whisper—or maybe a far cry—
and the bedroom was queasy with light the color
of lapis lazuli.

He lay there listening hard
till six, till seven, till eight . . .
At nine he remembered the bottle.
But nine, nine was too late.

"Don't take me!" cried the clozapine.
"Don't take me!" cried the pill.
By ten he was feeling restless,
with a whole day left to kill.

"Don't take me!" cried the clozapine.
"Yes, don't!" cried the medication.
And the bright yellow morning seemed suddenly edged
with a shady fascination.

Why should he go to his workplace?
Who was his supervisor?
He had a sickening feeling
that he was becoming wiser.

His room filled up with interest.
He had begun to think!
He thought of the knives in the kitchen
and the bottles under the sink.

He thought as he switched the stove on
or stood at his shaving mirror,
or reached for his belt in the wardrobe.
Thinking made things clearer.

Even the bedroom window,
the open window full of sun,
continually hinted
at something that should be done.

But he was crooked and useless.
He was a piece of shit.
And so, as everyone knew he would,
he failed to go through with it.

"Don't take me!" cried the clozapine.
"Don't take me!" cried the drug.
Just then, the telephone rang.
Just then, he ripped out the plug.

"Don't take me!" cried the clozapine.
"Don't take me!" cried the poison.
And the door of the house creaked open,
and the cellar door lilted and murmured,
and the garden gate groaned and yawned
and let a little noise in.

There, just outside his window,
lurked life like a cheap cartoon.
He shut the sash, locked it, and checked it,
and checked it all afternoon.

He lowered the blinds on that world,
no longer an agent of it,
but then, with one finger, pulled down a slat
and set his eye above it.

At first it was grimly amusing,
at last it was grimly grim,
to watch all those hunched, hurried people,
who made like they weren't watching him.

The neighbors were thinking out loud.
They knew he was no fucking good.
So he slumped on a stool in the corner
like a bad little snaggletooth should.

They called him a dirty pig, and laughed,
and said he shouldn't exist.
Sometimes they made a tsking sound,
or oinked at him, or hissed.

They hissed that he was to blame
for everything, and everyone knew it,
and that if he weren't such a pussy
he'd know what to do, and he'd do it.

He lay on his side on the rug
unable to move at all
except for his big right toe,
which dug and dug at the wall,
    which dug at the wall,
        which dug.

"Don't take me!" cried the clozapine.
"Don't take me!" cried the cure.
And they begged him to sew his mouth shut
just to make goddamn sure.

"Don't take me!" cried the clozapine.
"Don't take me!" cried the poison.
And the gate to the wicked city gaped,
and the gates of the temple screamed and screamed,
and the gates of the garden groaned and yawned,
and the gates of the ziggurat gabbled in grief
and sucked all life's sorrows and joys in.

His thoughts were advancing like wolves.
He lay still for an hour and a half,
then reared up onto his rickety legs
like a newborn calf.

Then   rug
                hall
                        stairs
porch
        stoop
                street
and the blacktop humanly warm
on the soles of his naked feet.

His walk was stiffened by fear,
but it took him where he was going,
into the terrible world
of children and daffodils growing,
    and friendly people helloing,
    and the Super out doing the mowing,
    and the two old sisters out in wool sweaters with their wrinkled
        cheeks pinkly glowing,
    and the pretty lady who would give birth by Christmas barely
        showing but showing,
    and the policeman helping to keep the lazy afternoon traffic
        flowing,
    and time itself slowing,
    and none of them, none of them knowing

that an odious axis was forming,
that it would not be controlled,

that schemes were afoot, that a foot
was a thing for a jackboot to hold,

that the street was a movie set,
that it was not warm and sunny,
that a creditor was calling
who could not be paid with money,

that the world was like a sliver
of iron held in the hand,
and his mind the lodestone above it
that made it stir or stand,

that the air was slowly changing
to a color they didn't know,
that he was a famous doctor
on a television show.

But what could he do? Even friends
would take these facts for lies,
and he couldn't tell who the enemies were,
though he felt the hot breath of their eyes,

so he kept his big mouth shut
and tried to play along,
and plowed down the street toward the coffeeshop
as if nothing at all were wrong.

He tried not to notice the numbers
painted on garbage cans.
He tried and he tried not to look
at the black unmarked sedans.

The coffeeshop smelled like coffee,
but it felt different inside.
A new waitress went by. She winked.
He kept his eyes open wide.

Everything screamed, "Run away!"
But he wasn't really there!
So he stood by the gumball machines
and smiled and tried not to stare.

"The power is yours!" said a T-shirt.
"Look for lightning!" reported the weather.
And the stranger who offered the Sports section said,
"It's all there, Chief. Just put it together."

Then wild-eyed out of the kitchen
stormed a small, hard old man,
shouting in a strange language
and waving a frying pan,

shoving him out the door
and into the chattering street,

shoving him, waving, shouting,
and pointing at his feet,
    at his bare, gray feet.

Then came the dark-blue uniform,
the badge glinting in the sun,
and the belt jangling like a storm trooper's
as the boots broke into a run.

"Take that!" cried the patrolman.
"Take that!" cried Johnny Law.
Street, knee, neck—
cuffs, curb, jaw.

And the flatfoot pushed him, bleeding,
into the sleek cruiser,
and he heard all the gawkers thinking
that he was a pig and a loser,

and his chin throbbed,
and the handcuffs ate at his wrist,
and he would be hacked into pieces soon
and would not be missed.

"Don't take me!" cried the victim.
"Don't take me!" cried the threat.

But the angry back of a head
was the only response he could get.

Lying on his side like a child
at the end of a big day,
he gazed up through the window
and watched it all slip away.

The little pen where they put him
had a toilet but no stall.
Here and there a message
scarred the gloss-white wall.

Time passed. But you couldn't tell it
on the trapped fly ticking the ceiling,
or the flickering light overhead,
or the sore on his chin congealing,
    or on the sound of the other pigs in the other pens, squealing.

When the men came, he was ready.
He talked. They took it all down.
And soon they were back in the cruiser,
on their way across town.

Then, into the mirrored building,
over the waxed lobby floors,

down miles of echoing hallways,
through the heavy brown doors,

into a humming beige room
with a bed and a river view,
and an outside lock, and jailers
who wore white instead of blue.

"Take that," smiled the doctor.
"Take that," smiled the nurse.
He pressed his lips still tighter,
and things got worse and worse.

"Please!" threatened the nurse.
"Please!" growled the doctor.
He raised his fists to cover his mouth,
but the nurse was too close, and he clocked her.

Now into the room came the big men,
who did not clamor or shout,
but pinned him with ease to the bed,
strapped him down, and went out.

And the doctor was there again, trailing
a spiderweb of cologne,
and the doctor told what would happen next,
in an expert monotone,

and the nurse took a needle
and emptied it into his arm,
and they both left, content
that he could do no more harm,

and he fought, and the straps cut his shoulders,
and he gnawed at his lip, and it bled,
and he held his bladder for three long hours,
then shivered and pissed the bed.

When the doctor came a fifth time,
it was long past dawn.
They'd found him a room, said the doctor,
gently restraining a yawn.

The next two days were sleep,
and words through a fine white mist.
Then he woke inside a machine
whose motion he couldn't resist:

"Tick-tock," said the clock.
"Creak, creak," said the bed.
"Drip, drip," said the sink.
"Throb, throb," went his head.
"Ho-hum," sighed the night nurse.
"Heh, heh," said the sicko.

"Why? Why?" screamed the patient.

"Howl, howl!" cried the psycho.

"Wolf! Wolf!" cried the boy.

"Gooble, gobble!" sang the freaks.

"Sa, sa!" cried the king.

"Tick-tock," went the weeks.

"Bang, bang," said the TV.

"Teeter-totter," went his brain.

"Click, click," went the checkers.

"Pitter-patter," went the rain.

"Bring, bring," said the pay phone.

"Snip, snip," went Fate.

"Jangle, jingle," went the keys.

"Clank, clink," went the gate.

"Bye-bye," said the nurse.

"Bye-bye," said the guard.

"Bar-bar," said the doctor.

"Baa, baa," said the lamb.

"My, my," said his mother.

"Boohoo!" cried Bo Peep.

"Bowwow," said the wolf.

"Baa, baa," said the sheep.

In the car away from that place,
the family had a pleasant chat.
He seemed fine again, and humble,
though his speech was oddly flat.

He said that the halfway house
where he would be residing
was located on a quiet block and had
green vinyl siding.

There, he met new people
and watched the television,
which did not watch him back
or speak to him with derision,

and he performed certain tasks
meant to teach certain skills,
and he got small checks from the government
to pay his enormous bills.

Each night he fell asleep,
and each morning he got up,
and he washed down his medicine
and squashed the paper cup,

feeling, in all, much better,
more in touch with common sense,
and also slightly bored
by the lack of consequence.

And the church bells rang
and a dinner bell tinkled
and the school bell tolled
and called all the good girls and boys in.
And all of them brought all their toys in.
And all of them swallowed their poison.

The News

What happened to today? Where did it go?
The raindrops dot the window and roll down.
One taps the glass, another, three at a time,
warping the view of black tree limbs and sky.
Long hush, quick crescendo. Wind leans on the sash.
Behind me in the shadows sleep two cats.
Nearby, like something small deposited
tenderly by a big wind on the bed,
my wife sleeps deeply through the afternoon.
The sky is gray. What color is the sky?
Rhinoceros? Volcanic dune? Moon dust?
Breast of a mourning dove? Gray butterfly?
Blank newsprint. There's no news, no news at all,
and will be none,
until, at long last, in the other room,
one light comes on, and then another one.

The Pay Phone

1982

A pay phone is ringing. It is twelve fifteen,
a balmy summer weeknight, no one around.
The ringing is both urgent and routine.
Loud, sharp, and even, it is the only sound.

It reaches to the fountain and marigold bed,
and down the dress-shop alley, and back again,
up past the darkened windows overhead,
past the green turret, past the finial. Then

the phone stops ringing. The air continues to ring.
When it, too, stops, the calm feels tentative.
But soon it's strong—too strong. It's sickening.
This is no place for human beings to live.

Then, once again, the pay phone starts to ring.
It will go right on ringing. No one at all
will hear this sound. No one is listening.
But someone must have some interest in this call.

The phone rings with enough force to be heard
two hundred miles and thirty years away.
And who is the caller? A mad lover spurred
by a broken promise? A client allowed to stray

from bed at Willing Helpers? Could it be
a desperate spouse, out to arrange a hit?
Or is it a wrong number? No. It's me,
at thirteen. Oh, how I wish I could answer it.

The Chemist

The chemist watched his daughter's Christmas play.
He saw her wise-man mustache come unstuck,
worm up and down, and down and off. He saw
her one line lost to coughing: "Gifts we bring Thee!"
And in his smile, and in his eyes, he showed
no changes. As he watched the rest, which starred
another person's daughter and a doll
embezzled from the church's Food and Toy Drop,
he marked with pleasure the attempt to conjure
the spirit of a moment special to them,
the pails of dry ice hidden by poinsettias,
and slowly, toward the flock, the low fog rolling.

Believe It

Hard to believe that, after all of it,
in bed for good now, knowing you haven't done
one thing of any lasting benefit
or grasped how to be happy, or had fun,

you must surrender everything and pass
into a new condition that is not
night, or a country, or a sleep, or peace,
but nothing, ever, anymore, for you.

Fanatics

Probing a hollow left by drugs or cancer,
or plain oblivion, where we all began,
they sound the space with questions someone can,
but most of us cannot, precisely answer,

and, hearing nothing, turn it inside out,
where—snubbing all we want the answers for,
missing how facts improve life, often more—
they stand beneath shared error, tired of doubt,
and, lost since their first, playact a second birth,
listening at the deep air, walls, and dust.

"What is our natural goodness worth?"

"Earth."

"What earthly power can we trust?"

"Rust."

"Then life is nothing, more or less."

"Less."

"All we can do is acquiesce."

"Yes."

Accepting the Disaster

Silence came first, not one of those silences
that afflicts a people facing years of hardship,
but the sound of republics of cities and villages
not noticing countless noticeable changes.
Some of us couldn't bear that kind of silence.
But we, ignoring our leaders' slick assurances
and the timid findings of our so-called experts,
finally heard our own small consciences,
and soon saw many signs of the disaster.

Crowds moved. The cities sang with grievances.
Squabbles occurred, and inconveniences,
and, before long, seditious skirmishes
rattled the squares and markets. Wantages
and strife spread inland. Some of the unrest
was calmed with salaried sports and danishes,
some with the help of a few quietuses.
And some was not calmed.
The rich, intrigued, watched from their terraces.
No one could reach the federal offices.
Old enemies reaffirmed old purposes

and hatched mad plots to milk our weaknesses.
Dry bones and ghosts dwelt in our allies' palaces.
We saw on the lampposts the blurred visages
of late and later disappearances
smiling from homemade flyers, and other posters
on post-office walls of shadowy grimaces,
and, at the curbside, bright encumbrances
of roses, lilies, tulips, irises.
So we tossed back our daily dosages
of purine alkaloid, faced our sadnesses,
and, every morning, shelved our essences
to join in battle with our mortgages
and the platinum plans of former Christmases;
then, past-due buggies to past-due cottages,
which held our sitting-apparatuses,
and white bread for baloney sandwiches,
and access to ten million circuses;
and, on our day off, stronger substances,
laughter and tears; then, premium mattresses
and capsule nothingness. But none of it
did anything to lessen the disaster.
The NGOs and global censuses
found that in wars and fatal illnesses
half the world ranked above world averages.
Millions succumbed to downlevel viruses,

millions to food and water shortages.
The west wind throbbed with doleful cadences,
salats, psalms, mantras, sutras, kaddishes.
Billions of women suffered miscarriages,
and billions carried imperfect fetuses.
What children lived behaved like savages,
grew hairy and surly, and erupted with blemishes,
and hard work bossed their hands with calluses.
We toiled, and we toiled, and we spent our dotages
becoming ostriches and walruses,
becoming glass, unwrapping lozenges.
Then came the ice shelves' promised breakages.
Undersea sensors captured sub-bass sounds
like the plaintive groans of slain leviathans.
Seas rose, and threatened to deluge our lowlands and isthmuses.
Our western forests turned to furnaces.
Equinoctial dust stopped up our sinuses.
Whole species vanished,
and, each month, one or two more languages.
And the temples burned with heartfelt pointless promises,
and people still swore by their household gods and goddesses.
And thinking, the most arcane of privileges,
was, like our relict dukes and duchesses,
the target of both pious homages
and stonings. But it clung in colleges,
and mandarins adorned our daises

and brought no help or joy. The sciences,
mainly applied, gave us appliances:
some that saved time, and some that killed time instead;
some that saved people, or people with certain advantages;
and some that killed people. And, like most businesses,
the arts attracted business geniuses,
though none knows what became of all the poets.
And the land convulsed and suffered cleavages,
and people moved rubble and listened at crevices,
stunned by the hush, and by assemblages
of rebar like wisteria in winter.
Water came, licking domes and cornices,
turned roads to rapids of minivans, livestock, lumber,
cholera, and bloated, similar carcasses;
and, leaving, took whole towns and parishes.
Our power plants enhanced these damages
with cesium and plutonium seepages.
Containment units hissed liked tortoises.
In other water, other leakages,
triggered by model business practices,
brushed miles of pure pelagic surfaces,
rock, leaf, eye, tongue, and wing, with sudden black.
And our small planet braved the ravages
of constant gamma-ray disturbances,
and it turned counterclockwise. Some of us
blamed aliens. And by small slippages

the moon was drifting.
The cosmos scattered. Its far provinces
were laden with prophetic stillnesses.
But, at the same time,
the whole void warped with interferences.
Time flickered. Measurements were biases.
All the stars, stones, and seas, the crocuses,
anemone, and Osage oranges,
ticks, hummingbirds, giraffes, and porpoises,
all homes, all temples, and all fortresses,
grandmothers, blacksmiths, chemists, princesses,
all safety pins, all diamond necklaces,
all music, memories, love, all fragrances,
all dialogue, and all occurrences
were a spray of senseless coalescences
and no more. Light, under whose auspices
the tidal pools first seethed with presences,
seemed to hold out against most challenges
to its constancy, though we could only see
a fraction of its sublime abundances.
Of darkness there was only the one kind,
and our pupils grew in it and eclipsed our irises.
But much worse, worst of all, were the silences.

Our children mock these reminiscences.
Trying to say what it was like is like

trying to teach the blind what darkness is.
True, some of our fears are just and some are specious,
and whether pain looks more like death or life
depends upon your personal preferences.
But years of days and shared experiences
have taught us to believe in the disaster.
And though nobody arrives with bandages
or canteens, or a plan, and though we sit
and wait as the sun slowly extinguishes,
even so, with time, and with a lot of patience,
finally we accepted the disaster.
And crowds moved. Cities sang with grievances.
The luckiest suffered a hundred comeuppances.
Long wars were waged by secret caucuses.
Flesh-eating plants grew in the provinces.
The rich, sobbing, were dragged from their terraces.
The temples burned with heartfelt pointless promises.
And the round wind came across the dry plains daily.

Shark's Tooth

At twilight on the beach I found a shark's tooth.
After three days of looking, and then not,
I stepped onto the sand, and there it was.
It happened as I twisted loose a shoe,
impatient to shake off the week's bad luck,
and looked up to appraise the sky and sea.
There was no reason it should catch my eye.
Except for the western wall of one far building
turned by the setting sun the color of Mars,
everything I could see was shades of blue.
The tooth was small, what kind of shark uncertain.
But there it was, dangerous, big enough
in a place of such unfathomable proportions
that I could seem, on balance, not much bigger.
It pointed at me from my open palm.
Was it an omen? The sky was getting darker.
I had been waiting patiently for something.
I held it in my hand, and I forgot it,
and dark-blue pelicans plied the dark-blue water,
where I could read the future of that sky.
A searchlight scanned the heavens and found the heavens.
The waves grew quiet. For a moment, foam

crackled like faraway applause. Red lights
blinked on the pier, which lay down lower beneath
a purple Asia of dissolving cloud.
The light grew eerier and eerier,
and, slowly, the horizon disappeared.

Since then, I've found my way back every year,
and I have searched for hours, both day and night,
from when the first soul comes to stare and stand,
made taller by her reflection on the shore,
until the tranquil miles of cool sand lie
dimpled with shadows, twenty thousand footprints,
only disturbed by my feet shuffling toward
the yearly-more-immaculate parapet
of sea grapes slowly darkening. And often
I hold my shark's tooth like a sort of charm,
a talisman to ward off superstition
and, through the one small stray coincidence,
bring sharply to my mind the thought of countless
coincidences that will never happen.
Each year, once more, I pass the place I found it.
I see it on the surface of the sand,
three or four paces from the wooden stairs,
where people made attentive by long views
pass by all day; where it had sat inside
the spreading shadow of a chirping dune

two minutes' walk at low tide from the water,
farther up than Poseidon normally rides;
where I might spend my life and never find one
poised on a peak between two child-sized footprints,
like a gift, or like bait, held out to me.

Notes

"Father Birmingham" is a fictional interpretation of material presented in the 2006 documentary film *Hand of God* by Joe Cultrera. The first line quotes, in full, an ad placed in several newspapers by the filmmaker's brother Paul, with the aim of finding others who, like him, had been victimized. The ad received many pertinent replies.

"Cold Turkey" echoes language from a chorus of Euripides' *Bacchae* as translated for the Harvard Classics by Gilbert Murray: "Will they ever come to me, ever again, / The long long dances . . . ?"

"The Orange Bottle" includes the phrase "piece of shit," which, though common, was suggested to me by an account of auditory hallucinations in *The Center Cannot Hold* by Elyn R. Saks. Saks's extraordinary memoir of life with schizophrenia also alerted me to the often undue use of restraints in psychiatric hospitals.

"Shark's Tooth" is dedicated to George Green.

Acknowledgments

Grateful acknowledgment is made to the following
publications, in which some of these poems first appeared:

The Battersea Review: "The Bowl," "Epitaph
Carved on a Shinbone," and "The News"

The Common: "Believe It" and "How Strange, How Sweet"

The Economy: "The Chemist" and "Psalm"

The New Republic: "The Forecast" and "The Smokestack"

The New Yorker: "Joe Pipe"

The New York Sun: "Sad Stories"

The New York Times: "The Polling Place"

The Paris Review: "At Home" and "The Library"

Parnassus: Poetry in Review: "Father Birmingham"

Poetry: "The Cement Plant," "Citation," "Cold Turkey,"
"The Crossroads," "Down in the Valley," "The Fair," "Fanatics,"
"Fire Safety," "Here," "The Hill," "The Orange Bottle,"
"The Professor," "The Sponge," and "Work Song"

River Styx: "Heard at the Men's Mission"
(as "At the Men's Mission")

Smithsonian: "The Pay Phone"

The Yale Review: "Elegy"

"The Dream Job" first appeared as a broadside published
by Shechem Press in its 2012 Artist Broadside Series.

"On the Way to Church School" first appeared (as "To Church
School") in *The Swallow Anthology of New American Poets*,
published by Swallow Press / Ohio University Press (2009).

The author would also like to thank the National Endowment
for the Arts for its indispensable financial support.